To

_____

From

_____

On

_____

GOLD
FRANK-INSIGHTS
& Mirth

Compiled by Michelle L. Geiman

Harold Shaw Publishers
Wheaton, Illinois

Cover design © 1996 by David LaPlaca
Compiled by Michelle L. Geiman

ISBN 0-87788-244-4

Library of Congress Cataloging-in-Publication Data

Gold, frank-insights, and mirth : a Christmas celebration book / compiled by Michelle L. Geiman. —
  Rev. ed.
    p.   cm.
  Rev. ed. of: I found it under the tree. ©1993.
  ISBN 0-87788-244-4 (paper)
  1. Christmas. I. Geiman, Michelle. II. I found it under the tree.
  GT4985.G64 1996
  394.2'663—dc20   96-24930
                                                              CIP

05 04 03 02 01 00 99 98 97 96
10 9 8 7 6 5 4 3 2 1

CONTENTS

ACKNOWLEDGMENTS

We have sought to secure permission for all copyrighted material in this book. Where copyright holders could not be located or acknowledgment was inadvertently omitted, the publisher expresses its regret.

Unless otherwise indicated, all Scripture quotations are taken from *The Holy Bible, New International Version*. Copyright © 1973, 1978, 1984 International Bible Society. Used by permission of Zondervan Publishing House. All rights reserved.

Scripture verses marked TLB are taken from *The Living Bible* © 1971. Used by permission of Tyndale House Publishers, Inc., Wheaton, IL 60189. All rights reserved.

Scripture quotations marked THE MESSAGE are from *The Message*. Copyright © 1993, 1994, 1995 by Eugene H. Peterson. Used by permission of NavPress Publishing Group.

Scripture quotations marked NASB are taken from the *New American Standard Bible*, © 1960, 1962, 1963, 1968, 1971, 1972, 1973, 1975, 1977 by The Lockman Foundation. Used by permission.

Scripture quotations marked NKJV are from *The New King James Version*. Copyright © 1979, 1980, 1982, Thomas Nelson Inc., Publishers.

CHRISTMAS
PAST &
PRESENT

Christmas Traditions

Whether we're enjoying that special break-fast Christmas morning or teasing children about Santa, we all have a need for traditions that make our hectic lives stable and familiar. And each family can create its own traditions; there are so many possibilities when it comes to having fun and sharing our time and attention with one another.

Traditions are formed delicately, sometimes without our realizing it. An experience that brings such joy that we want to repeat it in the same way soon becomes a family custom.

Cheri Fuller, Creating Christmas Memories: Family Traditions for a Lifetime

Sorry, no more Christmas cards left—only religious ones.

A London shop assistant, Christmas, 1950

When you pay twenty-five dollars for a Christmas tree, you've been trimmed more than the tree has.

Unknown

Her gifts at every door she leaves;
  She bends, and murmurs low,
Above each little face half-hid
  By pillows white as snow:
"And is He here?" Then, softly sighs,
  "Nay, farther must I go!"

Edith M. Thomas, Babushka (A Russian Legend)

Perhaps the best Yuletide decoration is being wreathed in smiles.

Unknown

Some of the ornaments are new this year. We collect musical instruments . . . miniature trumpets, lutes, violins. Some of the ornaments have belonged to the tree from the time our girls were born, left at this house to hang on the tree year after year. Some, like me, are a bit the worse for the wear. They were on my first tree. . . . It is more than a tree. It is an icon, for it recalls the tree of life.

Caryl Porter, Harvest from a Small Vineyard

The legend of the Christmas ship is common in countries facing the sea. The legendary ship might have a variety of cargo including gifts, Christian love, the Christmas spirit, or various personages.

Torstein O. Kvamme, The Christmas Carolers' Book in Song and Story

Those which come from the more intellectual of my friends have no longer anything peculiarly Christmas-cardy about them. . . . Nothing could be more refined. . . . Each card of them is a silent protest against the old kind of card.

J. C. Squire, On Christmas Cards

In some parts of England bees are popularly said to express their veneration for the nativity by singing, as it is called, in their hives at midnight on Christmas Eve.

John N. Then, Christmas: A Collection of Christmaslore

Real religion, the kind that passes muster before God the Father, is this:
Reach out to the homeless and loveless in their plight, and guard against
corruption from the godless world.

James 1:27, THE MESSAGE

With holly and ivy
So green and so gay
We deck up our houses
As fresh as the day

Unknown

But we can't afford the made-in-Japan splendors at the five-and-dime. So
we do what we've always done; sit for days at the kitchen table with scis-
sors and crayons and stacks of colored paper.

Truman Capote, A Christmas Memory

We all come home Christmas Eve, decorate the tree, open the presents,
eat ourselves into a coma, and it's all over.

Erma Bombeck, Family Ties That Bind . . . and Gag!

Our house is open, Lord, to thee;
Come in, and share our Christmas tree!
We've made each nook and corner bright,
Burnished with yellow candle-light.

But light that never burns away
Is only thine, Lord Jesus. Stay,
Shine on us now, our Christmas Cheer—
Fill with thy flame our whole New Year!

Luci Shaw, "Circled with Light," WinterSong

Green Christmas, white Easter.

German Proverb

Christmas cards in general and the whole vast commercial drive called
Xmas are one of my pet abominations; I wish they could die away and
leave the Christian feast unentangled.

C. S. Lewis, The Joyful Christian

"There's no need to worry about the size of your Christmas tree," intoned the Rev. George Hall last Sunday. "Whatever its height, in the eyes of your children, that tree will be 10 feet tall."

Burton Hillis, Better Homes and Gardens, December 1988

The Jesse Tree is an old tradition in some churches. The carrying out of this tradition involves: obtaining a tree branch or small evergreen tree on which to hang symbols, reading Scripture passages related to ancestors of Jesus, and making symbols which remind us of each of these persons.

Doris Williams and Patricia Griggs, Preparing for the Messiah

Traditions give us memories.

Doris Williams and Patricia Griggs, Preparing for the Messiah

A famous writer once sent Christmas cards containing nothing but twenty-five letters of the alphabet. When some of his friends admitted that they had failed to understand his message, he pointed to the card and cried, "Look! No L!"

Unknown

If a brother or sister is without clothing and in need of daily food, and one of you says to them, "Go in peace, be warmed and filled," and yet you do not give them what is necessary for their body, what use is that?

James 2:15-16, NASB

". . . see that you also excel in this grace of giving.

2 Cor. 8:7

Let us have leave to remember the festivities at Christmas, when the richest of us would club our stock to have a gaudy day, sitting round the fire, replenished to the height with logs, and the pennyless, and he that could contribute nothing, partook in all the mirth, and in some . . . of the feasting.

Charles Lamb, A Schoolboy's Holiday

Yet at Christmas the old traditions were observed and cherished. The well-remembered and well-loved customs were kept alive: the tree was cut and trimmed, the carols were sung, and the stockings were hung by the fire. Cherished memories warmed the hearts of those who were far from home.

Ruth L. Dieffenbacher

In the name of God our Creator we place our Christmas tree in our home. May its presence here speak to us of him without whom nothing was made and nothing can live.

Unknown

The tree is full of trimmings
And gifts for girl and boy;
The world is full of Christmas cheer,
Our hearts are full of joy.

Unknown

Keep the Christmas cards you receive on the dining room table in a stack. At each meal read the card which is on the top and see who it is from. As you pray to thank God for your food, pray for the person(s) and family who sent the card to you.

Elaine McCalla, Spring Hill Good Times

Something nice, the old firs believed, always happens to the trees that don't get trimmed.

Christopher Morley, The Tree That Didn't Get Trimmed

Yule, always a jolly season, was begun by bringing the Yule log, and followed by decorating with holly and ivy, singing and dancing. Sumptuous festivities lasted as long as the Yule log burned.

Torstein O. Kvamme, The Christmas Carolers' Book in Song and Story

Gifts and Giving

True gifts come from the heart of the giver, not just the pocketbook. Sometimes our favorite gifts cost nothing in terms of money, but are very expensive when we realize the personal cost involved. The original Christmas gift—God's own Son come to earth—was very costly to the heavenly Father. But the love we have through Jesus continues to be the highest gift that others can receive from us.

How many through the centuries have found shelter and care, fire and food, because the Christchild and his mother and the patient Joseph were crowded that first Christmas night out of the inn and lay in the stable!

Henry Van Dyke

"Do you give a gift just to get one in return?" Ma asked me quietly. "Is that what the spirit of kindness and giving is all about?"

Arleta Richardson, Treasures from Grandma

Give, and it will be given to you. A good measure, pressed down, shaken together and running over, will be poured into your lap. For with the measure you use, it will be measured to you.

Luke 6:38

Flowers leave part of their fragrance on the hand that gives them.

C. B. Eavey, 2500 Sentence Sermons

God's gift of love is a personal gift to each one. No one else can receive the gift for you. No one can express gratitude and worship for the gift for you.

J. Harold Gwyne, The Christmas Miracle

"Go break to the needy the sweet charity's bread;
For giving is living," the angel said.
"And must I be giving again and again?"
My peevish and pitiless answer ran.
"Oh no," said the angel, piercing me through,
"Just give till the Master stops giving to you."

Anonymous

Generosity and philanthropy are not inspired by the extent of your bank account. Unselfishness springs rather from your heart or disposition. Anyone who has not learned the joy of contributing when he or she has not a superabundance, he or she is not likely to part with anything, no matter how their bank account may expand.

B. C. Forbes

Thanks be to God for His indescribable gift!

2 Corinthians 9:15, NASB

Life is much like Christmas—you are more apt to get what you expect than what you want.

South African Bulletin

No one is so open-handed that he has nothing to give.

French Proverb

A Christmas gambol oft could cheer
The poor man's heart through half the year.

Sir Walter Scott, Old Christmastide

A candle lights others and consumes itself.

Traditional

On coming to the house, they saw the child with his mother Mary, and they bowed down and worshipped him. Then they opened their treasures and presented him with gifts of gold and of incense and of myrrh.

Matthew 2:11

Only that which I give away will last for eternity.

Paul Brandel, Speech at the Chicago Evening Club, November 23, 1975

If you are not generous with a meager income, you will never be generous with abundance.

Harold Nye

Keeping Christmas is good, but sharing it with others is much better.

Unknown

God loves a cheerful giver.

2 Corinthians 9:7, NKJV

If we bestow a gift or a favour and expect a return for it, it's not a gift but a trade.

Unknown

The holidays—Christmas in particular—are my favorite time of year. Why? Christmas is for sharing, and I love to "do" for others year round. Christmas just gives me another excuse! I spend weeks in the kitchen, baking for everyone's tastes. And then I get to give and give and give.

Michelle Geiman

Giving is the thermometer of our love.

Unknown

The spiritual King of the whole earth was born in the straw amid the oxen and asses. What an emphasis that gives to man's instinctive desire to show hospitality! And when we add to it Jesus' teaching "Inasmuch as ye did it unto one of these my brethren, even these least, ye did it unto me," the lesson is complete. Who can measure the effect of this example on man's generous but often denied instinct to show hospitality to his fellowmen!

Henry Van Dyke

I shop for Christmas gifts year round. Planning ahead with my gift giving helps me to focus on the person and getting him or her a uniquely suited gift, and takes away the anxiety of having to find gifts in crowded malls after Thanksgiving. Then I can truly focus on the *real* event and meaning behind Christmas.

Anonymous

Christmas is less than what it can be—and less than what it was intended to be—where gifts are given grudgingly, and where gifts are received without appreciation.

Unknown

And at home they're making merry 'neath the white
  and scarlet berry—
  What part have India's exiles in their mirth?

Rudyard Kipling, "Christmas in India"

Christmas won't be Christmas without any presents.

Louisa May Alcott, Little Women

If each individual will give of himself to whomever he can, wherever he can, in any way that he can, in the long run he will be compensated in the exact proportion that he gives. What will be your compensation?

Paul Brandel, Speech at the Chicago Evening Club, November 23, 1975

For unto whom much is given, of him much is required.

Luke 12:48

Selfishness is the greatest curse of the human race.

William Ewart Gladstone, Speech at Hawarden, 1890

The world asks: How much does he give? Christ asks, Why does he give?

John Raleigh Mott

An ungiving person does not live; he breathes, he eats, he sleeps, he gratifies his needs, but only exists until he has discovered the cleverly interwoven secret of life, giving of oneself. True giving is done without the slightest trace of expecting to receive. Is it only in giving that we ever receive? Perhaps in giving of oneself there is enough taken away to have room to receive.

Alice R. Pratt

God has given us two hands—one to receive with, and the other to give with. We are not cisterns made for hoarding—we are channels made for sharing.

Billy Graham

Happiness is not so much in having or sharing. We make a living by what we get, but we make a life by what we give.

Norman McQuen

No person was ever honored for what he received. Honor has only been the reward for what he gave.

Calvin Coolidge

The realization that he was in a position to give, that he could bring happiness easily to someone else, sobered him.

John Cheever, Christmas Is a Sad Season for the Poor

Unbar your heart this evening
And keep no stranger out,
Take from your soul's great portal
The barrier of doubt
To humble folk and weary
Give hearty welcoming,
Your breast shall be tomorrow
The cradle of a king.

Henry Van Dyke

Every good and perfect gift is from above, coming down from the Father
of the heavenly lights, who does not change like shifting shadows.

James 1:17

For pleasure hath not ceased to wait
    on these expected annual rounds;
Whether the rich man's sumptuous gate
    Call forth the unelaborate sounds,
Or they are offered at the door
    That guards the lowliest of the poor.

William Wordsworth, The Minstrels Played Their Christmas Tune

Most people apportion their giving to their earnings. If the process were reversed and the Giver of all were to apportion our earnings according to our giving, some of us would be very poor.

World Vision

What I kept, I lost,
What I spent, I had,
What I gave, I have.

Persian Proverb

Children

During this busy season, take time to share yourself and make memories with children—whether they're your own or those outside the family circle who need special care and happy moments, too. They grow up so quickly. Memories can become a child's most precious gift—and they don't require batteries!

Kids—what would we do without them? Children sweeten our days with unhesitating trust and affection and refresh our spirits with their enthusiastic approach to life and their vast curiosity for all things new and different. They're treasured gifts from God.

David and Annette LaPlaca, I Thought of It While Shaving

Living with a child is, literally, an incomparable experience. It's a gift that has made my life what it is today. I couldn't live without it.

Frank Ferrara, On Being a Father

[Jesus said,] "Let the little children come to me, and do not hinder them, for the kingdom of God belongs to such as these."

Mark 10:14

If you have lost your faith in yourself, just go out and get acquainted with a small child. Win his love and your faith will come stealing back to you before you know it.

Nick Kenny

Children are gleeful barbarians.

Joseph Morgenstern

In praising or loving a child we love and praise not that which is, but that which we hope for.

Goethe

Children are like little balls of energy. But that enthusiasm is the same quality that infuses their lives with warmth and light. Children have a way of making us embrace rather than shrink away from what life has to offer.

Betsy Lee, Making of a Miracle

Mother nature, in her infinite wisdom, has instilled within each of us a powerful biological instinct to reproduce; this is her way of assuring that the human race, come what may, will never have any disposable income.

Dave Barry, Dave Barry Turns Forty

On the bright face of a child one can capture
The old hope and faith we would seek to redeem . . .
The beauty we once saw, the sweet childish rapture
In the eyes of a small child aglow with a dream.

Ruth B. Field

[Daddy] said: All children must look after their own upbringing. Parents can only give good advice or put them on the right paths, but the final forming of a person's character lies in their own hands.

Anne Frank, The Diary of a Young Girl

Unconditional love is loving a child no matter what. No matter what the child looks like. No matter what his assets, liabilities, handicaps. No matter what we expect him to be, and most difficult, no matter how he acts.

Ross Campbell, How to Really Love Your Child

Sons are a heritage from the LORD, children a reward from him.

Psalm 127:3

Heredity is what a man believes in until his son begins to act like a delinquent.

Unknown

The Shepherds had an Angel,
  The Wise Men had a star,
But what have I, a little child,
  To guide me home from far,
Where glad stars sing together,
  And singing Angels are?

Christina G. Rossetti, The Shepherds Had an Angel

May God bless all the children everywhere at this time.

Leila T. Ammerman

Children need love, especially when they do not deserve it.

Harold S. Hulbert

God superintended your child's construction even down to the tips of his fingers. And just as surely as that child has his very own fingerprints, he has a lot of his very own other things as well—personality, perspective, and problems. He is as special as his fingerprints.

Cliff Schimmels, Oh No! Maybe My Child Is Normal!

If you make children happy now, you will make them happy twenty years hence by the memory of it.

Kate Douglas Wiggin

Children need your presence more than your presents.

Jesse Jackson

Children today are tyrants. They contradict their parents, gobble their food, and tyrannize their teachers.

Socrates

There is something wrong with our spiritual life when we do not love children, and when children do not love us.

T. J. Bach

Children are today's investment and tomorrow's dividend.

Unknown

'Twas the week before Christmas and all through the house, the children were bored; I cried "Help!" to my spouse. He said, "Get out the art supplies, paint, glue and twine. Let's keep them all busy for your sake and mine!"

Kathy Peel and Judie Byrd,
A Mother's Manual for Holiday Survival: Family Fun for Every Occasion

To show a child what has once delighted you, to find the child's delight added to your own, so that there is now a double delight seen in the glow of trust and affection, this is happiness.

J. B. Priestly

Dear Santy Claus, I want a tin kitching and a slad and some dolls jewelry. If you bring a tree put it in Lons room. Grampa says there is no room for trees this year so put it in Lons room. I want a red slad with pictures on it. I want a picture of raindeers on it. I hope the brownies will take this to you. I have been good. With love from Tootie Smith.

Sally Benson, Meet Me in St. Louis

Children are the only earthly possessions we can take with us to heaven.

Unknown

In every child who is born, under no matter what circumstances, and of no matter what parents, the potentiality of the human race is born again; and in him, too, once more, and of each of us, our terrific responsibility towards human life; towards the utmost idea of goodness, of the horror of error, and of God.

James Agee

Children are natural mimics. They act like their parents in spite of all our attempts to teach them good manners.

Unknown

One of the sweetest sights of all is a child clothed in pajamas, peeking wide-eyed around the corner at the Christmas tree and all the brightly wrapped gifts underneath.

Anonymous

Heredity is something you believe in if your child's report card is all A's.

Unknown

A child more than all other gifts
That earth can offer to declining man
Brings hope with it, and forward-looking thoughts.

William Wordsworth

By the time the youngest children have learned to keep the house tidy, the oldest grandchildren are on hand to tear it to pieces.

Christopher Morley

It is good to be children sometimes, and never better than at Christmas, when its mighty Founder was a child Himself.

Charles Dickens

And [Jesus] took the children in his arms, put his hands on them and blessed them.

Mark 10:16

Christmas Past

Smells from the kitchen, a special ornament, or a trip through the photo album can easily send us back to Christmases past. As we treasure those times and share them with others, we bring all of our separate life stories together. Children become better acquainted with Grandma, and friends are drawn closer into our family circle. And all the while, we are making memories of our own.

But is old, old, good old Christmas gone?

Unknown, An Hue and Cry after Christmas, 1645

Every Christmas afternoon, when all the gifts were opened, my dad would take us kids sledding. Now I honor that tradition by taking my grandkids sledding. Even though some of them are in college, they still come back for more!

Anonymous

Tradition. That's what's missing. . . . In my day, we'd get up on Christmas morning, take the sled, and go off in the woods looking for the yule log—biggest one we could find. We'd bring it home, singing at the top of our lungs.

Phyllis Reynolds Naylor, Whatever Happened to Christmas?

Jealously I guard my Christmas solitude.

George Gissing

One Christmas when I was a little girl I left a peanut butter sandwich and a glass of milk with a note for Santa. In the morning, the glass was empty, bites had been taken out of the sandwich, and the note was gone. I knew Santa had been there!

Mary Horner

Can it really be my duty to buy and receive masses of junk every winter just to help the shopkeepers?

C. S. Lewis, God in the Dock

One hopes that we may be allowed to have Xmas in peace.

Wipers Times, An Editorial on Christmas Day 1917

Every Christmas Eve, our family dresses up in old bathrobes, sheets, and whatever else we can find, and acts out the story of Christ's birth—complete with stuffed tigers, poodles, and lambs for the animals. The youngest child gets to be baby Jesus. Each year we take a group photo, laugh hysterically over everyone's created outfits, and share—as a family—in the joy and wonder of Jesus' birth.

Evangeline Cramer

Christmas is not what it was! Such is the perennial cry at Twelfth Night. The turkey, it is said, was tougher than usual; the New Year balls were less exciting, the singing of the choir feeble by previous comparisons. And thus it shall probably ever be. For to capture the excitement of our youth we must wait for our second childhood.

James P. Kenion

When I was a child, we celebrated Jesus' birthday with a specially made cake on Christmas morning. We sang "Happy Birthday to Jesus" and then dumped all our saved-up coins from our piggy banks onto the floor. We would count up the money and then go out and buy food for a needy neighbor, or put it into the offering plate at church the next week.

Vange Schock

My first Christmas away from my family was my junior year in college, when I was going to Austria. Christmas didn't *feel* right—I wasn't at home. And, to make things worse, Christmas didn't *look* right—there was no snow! On Christmas morning my parents surprised me with a phone call and made my whole day! It really made me realize how Christmas is for families and for being together.

Laura Mains

Home to laughter, home to rest,
Home to those we love the best.
Home where there is none to hate
Where no foes in anguish wait,
Where no jealous envious mind
Seeks with glee a fault to find,
Now the day is done and I
Turn to hear a welcoming cry.
Love is dancing at the door,
I am safe at home once more.

Unknown

Youth is given. One must put it away
like a doll in a closet,
take it out and play with it only
on holidays.

Unknown

In my day, you knew it was Christmas the minute Thanksgiving was over, because the smell of turkey was replaced with the fragrance of fruitcake and apple turnovers and all the butter cookies you could eat.

Phyllis Reynolds Naylor, Whatever Happened to Christmas?

The Christmas I was five my father taught me the nativity story from St. Luke and I said it from memory, at the seminary Christmas Eve service for children. Every time I hear the words "And there were in the same country shepherds, keeping watch over their flocks by night," that Christmastime returns to me. I hear my father's voice. I see the light from the kerosene stove that cast shapes like a lace doily on the ceiling of my father's study.

Caryl Porter, Harvest from a Small Vineyard

For years we put the Christmas tree in the parlor. It was the fanciest room in the old farmhouse—carpeted, wallpapered and curtained. It seemed fitting to celebrate the Master's birthday in the best room.

Jean Bell Mosley, "The Christmas in Mama's Kitchen"

Mother didn't expect to have anything to do with the Christmas pageant except to make me and my little brother Charlie be in it (we didn't want to) and to make my father go and see it (he didn't want to).

Every year he said the same thing—"I've seen the Christmas pageant."

"You haven't seen this year's Christmas pageant," Mother would tell him. "Charlie is a shepherd this year."

"Charlie was a shepherd last year, No . . . you go on and go. I'm just going to put on my bathrobe and sit by the fire and relax. There's never anything different about the Christmas pageant."

"There's something different this year," Mother said.

"What?"

"Charlie is wearing your bathrobe."

So that year my father went . . . to see his bathrobe, he said.

Barbara Robinson, The Best Christmas Pageant Ever

The Christmas Feast

It begins with a prayer and ends with sighs of contentment! Every culture has its special feasts. Perhaps this is because sharing a meal brings people together for relaxation and good conversation. The long-distance friends and relatives who come to eat Christmas dinner with us make it one of the most important meals of the year. And at probably no other time do we have such a wonderful variety of desserts!

I can almost smell the mouth-watering traditional Christmas dinner complete with orange and coconut ambrosia, sweet potato pie, turkey and giblet gravy. In my memory I can also still hear the traditional wrangling over who was going to get the coveted drumsticks!

Cheri Fuller, Creating Christmas Memories: Family Traditions for a Lifetime

The way to a man's heart is through his stomach.

Fanny Fern, Willis Parton

Two weeks before Christmas, my mom, sister, and I get together at one of our houses and bake up a storm. Our husbands go out together for dinner, and flour flies around the kitchen. At the end of that weekend we have all sorts of goodies to share—and to give away as gifts. We enjoy quality family time and reduce the stress of Christmas baking!

Anonymous

They will drink our healths at dinner—those who tell
  us how they love us,
And forget us till another year begone!

Rudyard Kipling, "Christmas in India"

One Christmas tradition I will never forget. Every Christmas morning, we would awake to the smells of fresh-baked candlebraid bread (our Norwegian neighbors called it Santa Lucia Crown). The youngest child in the family got to light the three red candles nestled in the bread and then carry it from room to room to wake up every other member of the family. When everyone was dressed, we had a floor picnic of candlebraid bread and orange juice on a Christmas tablecloth made by my grandmother.

Ray Carmen

It began the moment we sat down to dinner. Mr. Wopsle said grace with theatrical declamation—as it now appears to me, something like a religious cross of the Ghost in Hamlet with Richard the Third—and ended with the very proper aspiration that we might be truly grateful. Upon which my sister fixed me with her eye, and said, in a low reproachful voice, "Do you hear that? Be grateful."

"Especially," said Mr. Pumblechook, "be grateful, boy, to them which brought you up by hand."

Mrs. Hubble shook her head, and contemplating me with a mournful presentiment that I should come to no good, asked, "Why is it that the young are never grateful?"

Charles Dickens, Great Expectations

Leftovers are bits of food that are kept in the refrigerator until they are old enough to be thrown away.

Unknown

Christmas for me is the tastes and smells of spiced cider simmering in the Crockpot and fudge cooling on the stove.

Evangeline Cramer

The most disagreeable thing at sea is the cookery; for there is not, properly speaking, any professed cook on board. The worst sailor is generally chosen for that purpose. Hence comes the proverb, used among the English sailors, that "God sends meat, and the Devil sends cooks."

Benjamin Franklin

Little Jack Horner sat in the corner,
Eating a Christmas pie.
He put in his thumb, and pulled out a plum
And said, What a good boy am I!

Anonymous

One year my family created a sugar plum house big enough for neighborhood kids to walk through! We made the walls out of styrofoam insulation panels and then put homemade cookies and candy in baggies and covered the whole house with them. At the Christmas party everyone served themselves from the house.

Bonnie McCullough

There were pumpkin pies and a big bowl of whipped cream. (A surreptitious sample on the tip of the finger revealed it to be flavored with just the right amount of vanilla.) There were pickles (sliced cucumber, beet, and spiced crab apple), freshly baked buns, mashed potatoes, creamed carrots, and a large casserole of scalloped corn. Central to the whole feast was the huge turkey, beautifully browned. Grandma had just pulled it from the oven. The dressing was scooped into a serving dish and the gravy prepared.

Bob Artley, "A Family Christmas"

Walking to Hanley this afternoon I was struck by the orange-apple *cold* Christmas smell off the greengrocers' shops.

Arnold Bennet

"Turkey, cranberry sauce, mince pies and Christmas pudding," he said. "I can eat the lot. I do wish Mom would make chestnut stuffing the way I had it in Paris that time. Trouble is with Mom, she will insist on sticking to American cooking. She just can't get it into her head that maybe Old World cooking can be good too."

Marion Agnew

The best thing to put into a homemade pie is your teeth.

Unknown

Home is the place where you can try out new recipes that you wouldn't be able to try out on civilized folks.

Ramona Tucker

All families had their special Christmas food. Ours was called Dutch Bread, made from a dough halfway between bread and cake, stuffed with citron and every sort of nut from the farm—hazel, black walnut, hickory, butternut. A little one was always baked for me in a Clabber Girl baking soda can, and my last act on Christmas Eve was to put it by the tree so that Santa Claus would find it and have a snack.

Paul Engle, "An Iowa Christmas"

My father always had to work on the holiday, so we celebrated most of my childhood Christmas mornings without him. He was a closet gourmet cook, and especially loved to bake extravagant breads and other sweets during the winter holidays. So on Christmas morning there would be some treat already baked and ready for us. There were breads drizzled with frosting to be toasted under the broiler. Or pull-apart orange marmalade rolls for warming. All of them were tasty, full of candied fruit and nuts, braided or molded, and decorated with the perfection of a blue-collar worker who had always been an artist inside.

Vinita Hampton Wright

I feel a recipe is only a theme, which an intelligent cook can play each time with a variation.

Madame Benoit

Carols and Bells

Can there be a moment more perfect than hearing Christmas bells break out their song over the crisp morning landscape? Or sharing hot cider with the group of carolers who've come to your door?

Everyone knows what a carol is. At least in this highly stimulated, more than slightly terrifying season of giving and getting (without forgetting) one should certainly be able to recognize a Christmas carol if he heard one.

Robert Shaw, A Christmas Letter

The custom of ringing bells to announce the various festivals of the Christian Church is very old. Bells were first introduced during the 6th century and their use soon spread throughout Christendom.

Torstein O. Kvamme, The Christmas Carolers' Book in Song and Story

Music is one of the fairest and most glorious gifts of God.

Martin Luther

Is anyone happy? Let him sing songs of praise.

James 5:13

I had scarcely got into bed when a strain of music seemed to break forth in the air just below my window. I listened and found it proceeded from a band, which I concluded to be the waifs from some neighboring village. They went around playing under the windows—even the sound of waifs, rude as may be their minstrelsy, breaks upon the mid-watches of a winter night with the effect of perfect harmony.

Washington Irving, Sketch Book

On Christmas Eve, my dad and we two boys would head off into our woods, in search of the perfect tree. We'd sing carols at the top of our lungs, and jostle each other until one of us eventually ended up in the snowbank. But the best part was going home to hot chocolate and Bing Crosby on our old, scratchy phonograph.

Ray Carmen

The music in my heart I bore
Long after it was heard no more.

William Wordsworth, Rob Roy's Grave

O praise our Redeemer, all mortals on earth!
For this is the birthday of Jesus our King,
Who brought us salvation—His praises we sing!

From an old church gallery book discovered in Dorset, England

Art and music, splendidly equipped and full of skill, waits for an inspiration to use its powers nobly. Modern beneficence, practical and energetic, lacks too often the ideal touch, the sense of beauty. Both these priceless gifts, and who can tell how many more, may be received again when the heart of our doubting age, still cherishing a deep love of faith and a strong belief in love, comes back to kneel at the manger-cradle where a little babe reveals the philanthropy of God.

Henry Van Dyke

Special festivities were held for the children at Luther's home on Christmas Eve. At these annual festivities "From Heaven Above to Earth I Come" was one of the children's favorite songs. In singing the song, it was Luther's custom to have a student, dressed as an angel, sing the first seven verses. The children would then joyfully respond by singing the remaining verses, and on the last verse would leap about in a gleeful dance.

Torstein O. Kvamme, The Christmas Carolers' Book in Song and Story

After Mary learned that God had chosen her to be the mother of Jesus, she sang this song: "My soul glorifies the Lord and my spirit rejoices in God my Savior." Make these words your own prayer of rejoicing today.

Annette LaPlaca, How Long 'Til Christmas?

Christmas bells, Christmas bells,
  Chime forevermore,
Chime this happy Christmas Day
  Yes, of Him we all adore;
Christmas bells, Christmas bells,
  Tell o'er all the earth
Blessed tidings—sweet and true
  of the Saviour's wondrous birth.

Unknown

Every Christmas should begin with the sound of bells.

Paul Engle, "An Iowa Christmas"

Domestic and religious rite
Gave honour to the holy night:
On Christmas eve the bells were rung;
On Christmas eve the mass was sung.

Sir Walter Scott, Old Christmastide

From far away we come to you,
To tell of great tidings, strange and true.

Old English Carol

[I remember] the carol sung by night at that time of the year, which, when a young boy, I have so often laid awake to hear from seven (the hour of going to bed) till ten when it was sung by the older boys and monitors, and have listened to it, in their rude chaunting, till I have been transported in fancy to the fields of Bethlehem, and the song which was sung at that season, by angels' voices to the shepherds.

Charles Lamb, A Schoolboy's Holiday

Then God sent an angel from Heaven so high,
To certain poor shepherds in fields where they lie,
And bade them no longer in sorrow stay,
Because that our Saviour was born on this day:
Then presently after the shepherds did spy
A number of angels that stood in the sky;
They joyfully talked, and sweetly did sing,
To God be the glory, our Heavenly King.

Unknown

Then passed forth into the quiet night an ancient and time-worn hymn,
embodying a quaint Christianity in words orally transmitted from father
to son through several generations down to the present characters, who
sang them out right earnestly.

Thomas Hardy, Going the Rounds

The time draws near the birth of Christ:
  The moon is hid; the night is still;
  The Christmas bells from hill to hill
Answer each other in the mist.

Alfred Tennyson, "The Bells of Yule"

We are a caroling family. Every year, on New Year's Eve, we pack up the kids, grandmas, uncles, and spend an hour making fools of ourselves at the neighbor's houses. But we wouldn't miss it for anything!

Anonymous

Jesus himself gleams through
our high heart notes
(it is no fable).
It is he whose light
glistens in each song sung
and in the true
coming together again
to the stable,
of all of us: shepherds,
sages, his women and men,
common and faithful,
wealthy and wise,
with carillon hearts
and suddenly, stars in our eyes.

Luci Shaw, "Star Song," WinterSong

Families at Christmas

Christmas is one of the few times of the year when the extended family gets together. It's a time to keep schedules low-key, to provide lots of time just for sitting, visiting, and enjoying one another.

Home means many different things to as many different people, but at no time more than at Christmas does each of us long for and strive to go home, wherever it may be.

Ruth L. Dieffenbacher, Home for Christmas

In the home my grandmother created,
I find the beginnings of the love I have inherited.

Lois Wyse, Funny, You Don't Look like a Grandmother

'Tis a happy thing to be a father to many sons.

Shakespeare, King Henry VI

Happiness is like jam; you can't spread even a little without getting some on yourself.

Vern McLellan

The family altar would alter many a family.

Unknown

Thanks to changing family styles and the lack of support for children within the larger society, today's grandparents are often required to play different roles than they were expected to play in the past. You have to be part grandparent, part parent, part counselor, part confidant, and much more. . . . Your grandchildren also need more than was ever true for grandchildren in the past.

David Elkind, Grandparenting

Home's like Heaven!

Charles Dickens, A Christmas Carol

Home is where the college student, home for the holidays, isn't.

Laurence J. Peter

A smile costs nothing, but gives much. It enriches those who receive, without making poorer those who give. It takes but a moment, but the memory of it sometimes lasts forever. None is so rich or mighty that he can get along without it, and none is so poor but that he can be made rich by it.

Thomas C. Jones, The Joy of Words

To get the full value of a joy, you must have somebody to divide it with.

Mark Twain

Babies have a way of keeping mothers too busy for Christmas cookies.

Madeleine L'Engle, The Twenty-four Days Before Christmas: An Austin Family Christmas

In those early days of our country, home was where the family settled.

Ruth L. Dieffenbacher, "Home for Christmas"

Parents and grandparents hand down more than just brown hair, blue eyes, big noses, ears that stick out, etc. . . . They pass on a whole system of values, a whole picture of the world.

Annette Heinrich, Not a Hollywood Family

Home is the place where the great are small and the small are great.

Unknown

A real home is a gymnasium.
Unfortunate is the child who is prohibited from using his
   home for vigorous games because his mother doesn't
   want him to "mess up the house."
A real home is a workshop.
Blessed is the boy who has a kit of tools and is taught to
   use them.

Unknown

Home is the place where we are treated the best and grumble the most.

Unknown

As for me and my household, we will serve the LORD.

Joshua 24:15

A small girl gave this definition: "Relatives are people who come to dinner who aren't friends."

Unknown

There are no perfect families.

Kevin Leman

Every time a child is born, a grandparent is born, too. . . . For children, it is the gift of life. For grandparents, it is a gift of a new connection between all who have preceded them, and all who proceed from them.

Arthur Kornhaber and Kenneth Woodward, Grandparents/Grandchildren

Therefore encourage one another, and build up one another, just as you also are doing.

1 Thessalonians 5:11, NASB

Shut in from all the world without,
We sat the clean-winged hearth about.

John Greenleaf Whittier, Snowbound

Our jolly band came laughing, puffing, and stomping into the kitchen where Grandma and Mom had prepared a lunch of hot cocoa and leftovers from dinner.

Bob Artley, A Family Christmas

"For Christmas," a woman remarked to her friend, "I was visited by a jolly, bearded fellow with a big bag over his shoulder. My son came home from college with his laundry."

Unknown

The house of the righteous stands firm.

Proverbs 12:7

Pray for people in your family who do not understand the true story of Christmas.

Annette LaPlaca, How Long 'Til Christmas?

Home is the place where part of the family waits until the rest of the family brings back the car.

Unknown

Heap on more wood!—the wind is chill;
But let it whistle as it will,
We'll keep our Christmas merry still.

Sir Walter Scott, Marmion

When I was a boy of fourteen, my father was so ignorant I could hardly stand to have the old man around. But when I got to be twenty-one, I was astonished at how much he had learned in seven years.

Mark Twain

The most effective thing we can do for our children and families is pray for them.

Anthony T. Evans, Guiding Your Family in a Misguided World

CHRISTMAS IN OUR HEARTS FOREVER

The Christmas Spirit

We catch it as early as Thanksgiving, and it's one of the few things we catch at this time of year that we like to keep and share at the same time: the Christmas spirit!

And numerous indeed are the hearts to which Christmas brings a brief season of happiness and enjoyment.

Charles Dickens

The friendly stranger cannot refuse an admiring glance to this mystery of wealth and thrift and energy and good spirits.

Henry James, Paris, Christmas, 1876

At Christmas play and make good cheer,
For Christmas comes but once a year.

Thomas Tusser, The Farmer's Daily Diet, 1557

God bless the master of this house,
  The mistress also,
And all the little children,
  That round the table go,
And all your kin and kinsmen,
  That dwell both far and near,
I wish you a merry Christmas
  And a happy New Year.

Unknown

God rest you merry, gentlemen,
Let nothing you dismay;
Remember Christ our Saviour
Was born on Christmas Day.

Anonymous

During the war, when Mr. Weston was away, I was all alone at Christmas. I didn't have any Christmas dinner or a tree or anything. I just scrambled myself some eggs and sat there and cried.

John Cheever, Christmas Is a Sad Season for the Poor

I'm constantly amazed by the spirit of Christmas. It's the one time of year when the neighbor who normally hates me (he has good reason—my four-year-old launched a rock through his living room window; my two-year-old yanked up his prize-winning begonias) knocks on my door—with a *smile*—and hands me a plate of the most scrumptious looking and smelling cookies.

Anonymous

What is the Christmas spirit?
In the home, it is kindness.
In business, it is honesty.
In society, it is courtesy.
In work, it is fairness.
Toward the unfortunate, it is mercy.

Unknown

Normal people can always predict when the holidays are near at hand. There is an air of excitement, the smell of holly, the ringing of bells, the singing of carols. At our house, if we have measles, it must be Christmas.

Erma Bombeck, I Lost Everything in the Post-Natal Depression

When we throw out the Christmas tree we should be especially careful not to throw out the Christmas spirit with it.

Unknown

Sing hey! Sing hey!
For Christmas Day
Twine, mistletoe and holly
For friendship glows
In winter snows,
And so let's all be jolly.

Unknown

There is a deep note of human pathos in the simple narrative of the events of the first Christmas—something infinitely affecting that moves the heart far more profoundly than resounding and eloquent words. The elemental desires and relations of the human soul are touched: the unutterable yearning of the heart for salvation; the simplicity of the greatest events; the meekness of mankind at the best; the smallness of beginnings that have the most far-reaching consequences.

Henry Van Dyke

I will honor Christmas in my heart, and try to keep it all the year.

Charles Dickens, A Christmas Carol

Happy Christmas to all, and to all a good night!

Clement Clarke Moore, A Visit from St. Nicholas

Joy is not in things. It is in us.

Megiddo Message

I don't think that the real Christmas spirit can be triggered by a couple of evergreen wreaths or by last year's Santa even when he's perched on a stoplight. . . . There's something missing when those things stir a feeling which we call the Christmas spirit.

Charles S. Mueller, The Christian Family Prepares for Christmas

Good King Wenceslas looked out
On the feast of Stephen,
When the snow lay round about,
Deep and crisp and even.

John Mason Neale, Good King Wenceslas

There's a lot more to Christmas than Santa Claus. There's also the spirit of kindness and giving.

Arleta Richardson, Treasures from Grandma

But you, Bethlehem, in the land of Judah,
are by no means least among the rulers of Judah;
for out of you will come a ruler
who will be the shepherd of my people Israel.

Matthew 2:6

The people walking in darkness
have seen a great light;
on those living in the land of the shadow of death
a light has dawned.

Isaiah 9:2

Christmas candles in the window
Shine out in the dark of night,
And the many people passing
Look and see their shining light.
When they see bright candles burning,

Doesn't matter where they are,
They may stop and think with gladness
Of the light of Bethlehem's star,
As it shone through lonely darkness
On the pathways men had worn,
Brightening all the world around it
At the time when Christ was born.

Unknown

God save you all, this Christmas night.

Sandys Wason

At Christmas I no more desire a rose
Than wish a snow in May's newfangled mirth;
But like of each thing that in season grows.

Shakespeare, Love's Labour's Lost

A voice of one calling:
"In the desert prepare
    the way for the LORD;
make straight in the wilderness

a highway for our God.
Every valley shall be raised up,
   every mountain and hill made low;
the rough ground shall become level,
   the rugged places a plain.
And the glory of the LORD will be revealed,
   and all mankind together will see it."

Isaiah 40:3-5

This will be a sign to you: You will find a baby wrapped in cloths and lying in a manger.

Luke 2:12

The cheerfulness and exuberant joy of Christmas paint the months of November and December with loud reds and fragrant greens. Yet in the midst of all this explosion of color, may our hearts turn toward the more "earthy" colors: God's birth among the straw and gentle animals, and his continuing presence with us today.

Ramona Tucker

Baby Jesus

The birth of a child should always be precious to us. And birth itself is possibly the greatest miracle of human existence. But were it not for one special birth, an even greater miracle would not be possible—spiritual rebirth, through the life, death, and resurrection of Jesus Christ, that "babe in the manger."

For a child will be born to us, a son will be given to us;
And the government will rest on His shoulders;
And His name will be called Wonderful Counselor, Mighty God,
Eternal Father, Prince of Peace.

Isaiah 9:6, NASB

The little Jesus came to town;
With ox and sheep He laid Him down;

Peace to the byre, peace to the fold,
For that they housed Him from the cold!

Lizette Woodworth Reese, A Christmas Folk Song

Blessed babe! what glorious features—
  Spotless fair, divinely bright!
Must He dwell with brutal creatures?
  How could angels bear the sight?

Isaac Watts, A Cradle Hymn

"You will conceive in your womb and bring forth a son, and shall call His name Jesus. He will be great, and will be called the Son of the Highest; and the Lord God will give Him the throne of His father David. And He will reign over the house of Jacob forever, and of His kingdom there will be no end."

Luke 1:31-33, NKJV

The birth of Jesus is the sunrise of the Bible. Towards this point the aspirations of the prophets and the poems of the psalmists were directed as the heads of flowers are turned towards the dawn. From this point a new day began to flow very silently over the world—a day of faith and freedom, a day of hope and love.

Henry Van Dyke

Waye not His cribb, his wodden dishe,
Nor beastes that by Him feede;
Waye not His mother's poore attire,
Nor Josephe's simple weede.
The stable is a Prince's courte,
The cribb his chaire of State;
The beastes are parcell of His pompe,
The wodden dishe His plate.

Robert Stowell

The virgin will be with child and will give birth to a son, and they will call him "Immanuel"—which means, "God with us."

Matthew 1:23

For in a manger bed,
Cradled we know,
This is the irrational season

When love blooms bright and wild.
Had Mary been filled with reason
There'd have been no room for the child.

Madeleine L'Engle, "After Annunciation," The Weather of the Heart

Nativity poems are of every century and decade; their poets do not borrow, but re-interpret.

George Y. Justin

While they were there, the time came for the baby to be born, and she gave birth to her firstborn, a son. She wrapped him in cloths and placed him in a manger, because there was no room for them in the inn.

Luke 2:6-7

When we remember the high meaning that has come into human life and the clear light that has flooded softly down from the manger-cradle in Bethlehem of Judea, we do not wonder that mankind has learned to reckon history from the birthday of Jesus, and to date all events by the years before or after the Nativity of Christ.

Henry Van Dyke

Without thee all of us were undone;
  Our love is won
  By thine, O Son of Mary.

Unknown, In the Holy Nativity of Our Lord God

His name shall endure forever, and all men shall be blessed in Him.

Unknown

Ah! dearest Jesus, Holy Child,
Make Thee a bed, soft, undefil'd,
Within my heart, that it may be
A quiet chamber kept for Thee.

Martin Luther, A New Year's Carol

Christ came to Bethlehem,
Long, long ago.

Anonymous

"She will give birth to a son, and you are to give him the name Jesus,
because he will save his people from their sins."

Matthew 1:21

Hail to thee, King of Jerusalem!
Though humbly born in Bethlehem,
A sceptre and a diadem
  Await thy brow and hand!
The sceptre is a simple reed,
The crown will make thy temples bleed,
And in thy hour of greatest need,
  Abashed thy subjects stand!

Henry Wadsworth Longfellow, The Nativity

Then Simeon blessed them and said to Mary, his mother: "This child is destined to cause the falling and rising of many in Israel, and to be a sign that will be spoken against, so that the thoughts of many hearts will be revealed. And a sword will pierce your own soul too."

Luke 2:34-35

Jesus on His Mother's breast
  In the stable cold,
Spotless Lamb of God was He,
  Shepherd of the fold:

Let us kneel with Mary Maid,
  With Joseph bent and hoary,
With Saint and Angel, ox and ass,
  To hail the King of Glory.

Christina G. Rossetti, Before the Paling of the Stars

I sing the birth was born to-night,
The author both of life and light;
  The angels so did sound it,
And, like the ravished shepherds said,
Who saw the light, and were afraid,
  Yet searched, and true they found it.

Ben Johnson, Wexford Carol

On this day, Earth shall ring
With the song children sing
To the Son, Christ our King,
Born on earth to save us,
Him the Father gave us.

Unknown, Ideo Gloria in Excelsis

Of the offspringe of the gentleman Jafeth come Abrahan, Moses, Aaron, and the Prophets, also the King of the right line of Mary, of whom that gentle-man Jesu was borne.

Julia Berners

What can I give Him
Poor as I am;
If I were a shepherd,
I'd give Him a lamb.
If I were a wise man,
I would do my part.
But what can I give Him?
I will give my heart.

Christina G. Rossetti, "My Gift"

Keeping Christ in Christmas

How easy it is, what with presents to buy, food to prepare, houses to clean, Christmas programs to attend, and parties to go to, to forget the reason for our joy and hope. Keeping Christ central to our celebrations can save us from "holiday burnout." True Christmas joy will sustain us through the darkest, coldest days of winter.

"Christmas is Christ's birthday. Keep it that way!" Whenever he said this, the congregation sympathetically nodded its agreement, assumed a position of pious horror at the terrible things the world was doing during the Christmas season, and then went right on encouraging these abuses by their wholehearted participation.

Charles S. Mueller, The Christian Family Prepares for Christmas

Christian life consists of faith and charity.

Martin Luther

The coming of Christ by way of a Bethlehem manger seems strange and stunning. But when we take Him out of the manger and invite Him into our hearts, then the meaning unfolds and the strangeness vanishes.

C. Neil Strait

He [Tiny Tim] told me, coming home, that he hoped people saw him in the church, because he was a cripple, and it might be pleasant to them to remember upon Christmas Day, who made lame beggars walk and blind men see.

Charles Dickens, A Christmas Carol

To Bethlehem our hearts, star led
  From wanderings far and wild,
Turn to a lowly cattle-shed
  And kneel before the Child.

We come from deserts, pitiless
  With lonely human pride;
And from the howling wilderness
  Where dread and hate abide.

Touched by his hand we find release
  From heavy griefs and fears:
Our hearts are lifted up with peace
  And purified by tears.

Ah Saviour dear! Thou Holy Child,
  What power is thine to heal
Our broken hearts, our wills defiled,
  When at thy feet we kneel.

Grant us thy grace no more to roam,
  But, following thee alway,
Find Bethlehem in every home,
  The whole year Christmas Day.

Henry Van Dyke

As light is a symbol of our abundant, eternal life, let us follow him who
is the one true Light of the World. May the light of Christmas shine on
our hearts through the year to come.

Leila T. Ammerman

Christ is no longer the baby of Bethlehem as so many people seem to think, but He is the Saviour of the world! He came to show men their sins, but not only to show them but also to be the One who could remove them and give . . . abundant life!

Unknown

For God was pleased to have all his fullness dwell in him, and through him to reconcile to himself all things, whether things on earth or things in heaven, by making peace through his blood, shed on the cross.

Colossians 1:19-20

The gods lie cold where the leaves lie gold,
   And a Child comes forth alone.

G. K. Chesterton, A Child of the Snows

For a moment God tore open the heavens and let the angelic ecstasy break down on the ears of men. It was the day that marked the beginning of the end for Satan and his power and set the Light of the world firmly in the midst of sin's inky blackness. It was a day eagerly anticipated by the prophets of old and joyfully remembered by His people.

Charles S. Mueller, The Christian Family Prepares for Christmas

Can we think of a crib without a cross, or a cross without a crown? I think not. All are one, and one cannot be without the other two—or so it seems to me.

Jill Briscoe, "Christmas Now," Heartbeat

Wherever Christmas is truly experienced and kept, it will be in the hearts and homes and churches of those who have borrowed their light from the Christ Child; who have lighted their altar lamps of love, devotion and worship with the candles from Bethlehem.

J. Harold Gwyne, The Christmas Miracle

Could every time-worn heart but see Thee once again,
A happy human child, among the homes of men,
The age of doubt would pass—the vision of Thy face
Would silently restore the childhood of the race.

Henry Van Dyke

How proper it is that Christmas should follow Advent.—For him who looks towards the future, the manger is situated on Golgotha, and the cross has already been raised in Bethlehem.

Dag Hammarskjöld, Markings

For you know the grace of our Lord Jesus Christ, that though He was rich, yet for your sake He became poor, that you through His poverty might become rich.

2 Corinthians 8:9, NASB

Since the children have flesh and blood, he too shared in their humanity so that by his death he might destroy him who holds the power of death—that is, the devil—and free those who all their lives were held in slavery by their fear of death.

Hebrews 2:14-15

We all need to light our candles at the fountain of light—divine love. Love to God and man is the light of the soul.

J. Harold Gwyne, The Christmas Miracle

So remember while December
Brings the only Christmas day,
In the year let there be Christmas
In the things you do and say.

Anonymous

Remember what Christ taught and let his words enrich your lives and make you wise, teach them to each other and sing them out in psalms and hymns and spiritual songs, singing to the Lord with thankful hearts.

Colossians 3:16, TLB

Jesus Christ was born *into* this world, not *from* it. He did not emerge out of history; He came into history from the outside. Jesus Christ is not the best human being the human race can boast of—He is a Being for whom the human race can take no credit at all. He is not man becoming God, but God Incarnate—God coming into human flesh from outside it. His life is the highest and the holiest entering through the most humble of doors. Our Lord's birth was an advent—the appearance of God in human form. This is what is made so profoundly possible for you and for me through the redemption of man by Jesus Christ.

Oswald Chambers, My Utmost for His Highest

There are some of us . . . who think to ourselves, "If I had only been there! How quick I would have been to help the baby. I would have washed His linen. How happy I would have been to go with the shepherds to see the Lord lying in the manger!" Yes, we would. We say that because we know how great Christ is, but if we had been there at that time; we would have done no better than the people of Bethlehem. . . . Why don't we do it now? We have Christ in our neighbor.

Martin Luther

And this I know, if only from hearsay . . . these things . . . were done, BECAUSE OF THE CHILD.

David Jones

It is here, in the thing that happened at the first Christmas, that the most profound unfathomable depths of the Christian revelation lie. God became man; the divine Son became a Jew; the Almighty appeared on earth as a helpless human baby, unable to do more than lie and stare and wriggle and make noises, needing to be fed and changed and taught to talk like any other child. And there was no illusion or deception in this: the babyhood of the Son of God was a reality. The more you think about it, the more staggering it gets. Nothing in fiction is so fantastic as this truth of the incarnation.

J. I. Packer, Your Father Loves You

That's some of what this day we call Christmas means. It is the remembrance of God's greater answer to man's very great need.

Charles S. Mueller, The Christian Family Prepares for Christmas

The beginning shall remind us of the end
And the first Coming of the second Coming.

T. S. Eliot

Christmas Prayers

Christmas is a season of remembering all that God has graciously done for us. We can best express our gratefulness for his goodness through prayer. Thank him for his mercy and love all through the year, and especially during this blessed season.

O Almighty God, who by the birth of thy Holy One into the world didst give thy true light to us to believe in the mystery of his incarnation and hast made us partakers of the divine nature, so in the world to come we may ever abide with him, in the glory of his kingdom; through the same Jesus Christ our Lord. Amen.

Unknown

Praise be to the Lord, the God of Israel,
because he has come and has redeemed his people.

Luke 1:68

O God, who hast made this most sacred night to shine with the illumination of the True Light, grant, we beseech thee, that, as we have known the mystery of that Light upon earth, we may also perfectly enjoy it in heaven; through the same Jesus Christ our Lord. Amen.

Gelasian Sacramentary

We yearn, our Father, for the simple beauty of Christmas—for all the old familiar melodies and words that remind us of that great miracle when He who had made all things was one night to come as a Babe, to lie in the crook of a woman's arm. Before such a mystery we kneel, as we follow the Shepherds and Wise Men to bring You the gift of our love—a love we confess that has not always been as warm or sincere or real as it should have been. But now, on this Christmas Day, that love would find its Beloved, and from You receive the grace to make it pure again, warm and real. We bring You our gratitude for every token of Your love. Amen.

Peter Marshall

My soul glorifies the Lord and my spirit rejoices in God my Savior . . . for the Mighty One has done great things for me—holy is his name.

Luke 1:46-49

Lord Jesus, for whose sake all motherhood is holy, and since whose coming the little children are first in the kingdom of thy Father, come to every household and family that loves thee on this Christmas Eve. Speak comforting things to the heart of every mother, and take the little children into thine arms, O Christ. Let every Christmas gift be a reminder of thee, and let thy Name be spoken softly in every home. Lord Jesus, hear; Lord Jesus, come; and light this home with Christmas love. Amen

Unknown

Dear God, the years of waiting for the promised Savior are over! We rejoice with the shepherds. We join the angels' songs of praise. Give us faith to live always as your people. Amen.

Nancy Vignec, Wreath of Light: Devotions for Families Using the Advent Wreath

We yearned for a Light to burst through the darkness of our sins to make us spotless and clean again. . . .We needed a living love to show us kindness, strength, and how to care well for one another. And You came! Thank You, Son of God. Amen.

Sharon Lee, Our Christmas Handbook

Almighty God, we give Thee thanks for the mighty yearning of the human heart for the coming of a Saviour, and the constant promise of Thy Word that He was to come. In our own souls we repeat the humble sighs and panting aspirations of ancient men and ages, and own that our souls are in darkness and infirmity without faith in Him who comes to bring God to man and man to God. We bless Thee for the tribute that we can pay to Him from our very sense of need and dependence, and that our own hearts can so answer from their wilderness, the cry, "Prepare ye the way of the Lord." In us the rough places are to be made smooth, the crooked straight, the mountains of pride brought low, and the valleys of despondency lifted up. O God, prepare Thou the way in us now, and may we welcome anew Thy Holy Child. Hosanna! blessed be he who cometh in the name of the Lord. Amen.

Samuel Osgood

The day of Joy returns, Father in Heaven, and crowns another year with peace and good will. Help us rightly to remember the birth of Jesus, that we may share in the song of the angels, the gladness of the shepherds, and the worship of the wise men. Close the doors of hate and open the doors of love all over the world. Let kindness come with every gift and good desires with every greeting. Deliver us from evil, by the blessing that Christ brings, and teach us to be merry with clean hearts. May the Christmas morning make us happy to be thy children and the Christmas evening bring us to our bed with grateful thoughts, forgiving and forgiven, for Jesus' sake—Amen.

Henry Van Dyke, "A Prayer for Christmas Morning"

A Christmas Meditation

Keeping Christmas

He that regardeth the day, regardeth it unto the Lord.
Romans 14:6, KJV

It is a good thing to observe Christmas day. The mere marking of times and seasons, when men agree to stop work and make merry together, is a wise and wholesome custom. It helps one to feel the supremacy of the common life over the individual life. It reminds a man to set his own little watch, now and then, by the great clock of humanity which runs on sun time.

But there is a better thing than the observance of Christmas day, and that is, keeping Christmas.

Are you willing to forget what you have done for other people, and to remember what other people have done for you; to ignore what the world owes you, and to think what you owe the world; to put your rights in the background, and your duties in the middle distance, and your chances to do a little more than your duty in the foreground; to see that your fellow-men are just as real as you are, and try to look behind their faces to their hearts, hungry for joy; to own that probably the only good reason for your existence is not what you are going to get out of life, but what you are going to give to life; to close your book of complaints against the management of the universe, and look around you for a place where you can sow a few seeds of happiness—are you willing to do these things even for a day? Then you can keep Christmas.

Are you willing to stoop down and consider the needs and the desires of little children; to remember the weakness and loneliness of people who are growing old; to stop asking how much your friends love you, and ask yourself whether you love them enough; to bear in mind the things that other people have to bear on their hearts; to try to understand what those who live in the same house with you really want, without waiting for them to tell you; to trim your lamp so that it will give more light and less smoke, and to carry it in front of you so that your shadow will fall behind you; to make a grave for your ugly thoughts, and a garden for your kindly feelings, with the gate open—are you willing to do these things even for a day? Then you can keep Christmas.

Are you willing to believe that love is the strongest thing in the world—stronger than hate, stronger than evil, stronger than death—and that the blessed life which began in Bethlehem nineteen hundred years ago is the image and brightness of the Eternal Love? Then you can keep Christmas.

And if you keep it for a day, why not always?

But you can never keep it alone.

Henry Van Dyke